FROM THE HEART

Poetry birthed from the altar of life…

ELEANOR GEORGE

From the Heart: Poetry birthed from the altar of life…
© 2022 by Eleanor George

Unless otherwise indicated, all Scripture quotations in this volume are from the King James Version of the Bible.

ISBN 978-1-953526-38-0

Second printing

TaylorMade Publishing, LLC has allowed this work to remain exactly as the author intended, verbatim, without editorial input.

TaylorMade Publishing

Published by TaylorMade Publishing, LLC of Florida
www.TaylormadePublishingFL.com
Florida

Printed in the United States of America

Dedicated to my wonderful parents
Anna & Alphonso

To my beloved children
Dejshona, Michael & Matthew

To all the members of the body of
Jesus Christ on earth

And especially to those who struggle without a voice…

TABLE OF CONTENTS

FOREWORD

In this incredible time in our society in the western culture, where we have been seduced into believing we have the power to reshape our reality into whatever form suits us, it is refreshing to find individuals with the courage to take a hard stare at the core of their inner person, and instead of searching for the quick fix, and the superficial make over, opt to begin the hard work of tearing down for the purpose of building up. This kind of personal renovation requires not only the willingness to initiate such a project, but also the determination to gain understanding as to what, where and how to proceed in this life changing process.

Eleanor George is such a person, who after many wrong turns going off the on ramp, is willing to share her journey in the beautiful lyrical fashion that only a truly gifted individual would dream to attempt. As you move through this work, you will share both pain and healing, and defeat turned to victory. As Eleanor continues her spiritual journey with a keen eye for the prize you will find her transparency is an invitation to the reader to join her in daring to dream for a life of change and conquest. It is a call to look inward with an honest eye, but to do so while acknowledging the presence of God that will insure the success of the enterprise.

Eleanor's success in sharing with you this writing, is a testimony to all of us that "we can do all things through Christ, which strengthen us."

Bishop Rev. Carlton T. Brown,
Senior Pastor
Bethel Gospel Assembly
Harlem, NY

INTRODUCTION

Where there is no vision, the people perish...
(Proverbs 29:18a)

This book was written as a result of a deep vision God impressed on my heart. Many of the poems in this book have not just inspired me but kept me alive during dark periods of my life. My hope is that these words will bring you comfort, hope and new perspectives...

I have discovered that "Poetry is the language of life."
Through poetry man expresses his innermost feelings, drive, dreams, hopes and the gamut of human emotions. **From the Heart Poetry birthed on the altar of life** *is a collection of poetry that reflects my life experiences as a Christian, urban, black woman, single mother and educator. I have believed deeply, loved completely, observed and wondered about life relentlessly.*

However, my life has been filled with sunshine and storms. Consequently, through an unending relationship with my creator—the Lord Jesus Christ—I have discovered a wealth of unconditional love and hope which helped and helps me navigate my sometimes difficult journey. As you read you will experience my life filled with challenges, struggles, understanding and triumphs. Through the vehicle of poetry you will feel my pain and rejoice with my joys. You may discover the intents and reflections of your own heart within the revealing words, the poetry of my soul, the language of love and the reflections of life...

So sit back and relax as you experience the unforgettable, unfathomable journey of a unique—yet familiar—life of a real woman, as you read and savor **From The Heart!**

By Eleanor Denise George

For I know the plans I have for you…

(Jeremiah 29:11)

*For the vision is for an appointed time
…though it may tarry
wait for it
it will surely come…*

(Habakkuk 2:3)

FAITH & LIFE: THE STRUGGLE

Many are the afflictions of the righteous
But the LORD will deliver them out of
them all.

Psalm 34:19

Being confident of this, that he who began a good work in you
will carry it on to completion until the day of Jesus Christ
Philippians 1:6

REASON VS. FAITH

There are things in life we may never understand:
Situations, tragedies, strengths, triumphs, failures, people,
ourselves, life…death.

Our Internet activated—yet finite minds—unable to fathom
the depths
To answer the unanswerable questions our quest,
Frustration intense, God's sovereignty as Alpha & Omega,
Reason refuses to rest;
Unable to accept that only an infinite God knows why
To understand with our last breath the human mind will try.

Omniscient God knows what we will never know
Omnipotent God has power to see what we cannot imagine
Omnipresent God is there when in our humanness we
despair,
Because we don't understand…What does not make sense.

So God imparted into mankind Divine Faith
That steps in when Reason fails;
Faith that God's Word is reliable and true,
Faith that says despite it all—Father I believe You:
I don't understand, yet I believe,
Faith propels me;
All Things Work Together For Good finally understood.

Life survives.

Another moment in time…

Hope is Born…

From Faith…

FORGIVEN

Lord was that really me?
No Lord that just can't be!
Oh God, it was me in sin,
I feel so torn up within.
Jesus forgive me if you will,
Speak, whisper to my heart, "Peace be still…"
Give me the faith to accept your forgiveness and love,
Because it's coming from the Almighty, Compassionate,
one above.

You tell me in your Word,
That is was for me you died;
That all my sins with you were crucified.
I gladly receive your forgiveness,
And boldly come to your throne of grace,
Seeking only the Master's face.

Jesus. It's so comforting—by faith
To look into your loving face,
When I look into your face I see,
The only one who died for me;
I see forgiveness in your eyes,
Out comes a teardrop of heartache
While for me you cry,
All over your face I see sweet peace,
Oh how I pray your peace in me will increase.

Yet He still outstretches his hand,
With that gesture He says, "Come I understand,"
I know that my Jesus loves and cares,
The former doubt in my heart begins to disappear.

Jesus is so close that I can feel him,
So soothing that I can unwind,
I'm safe—through repentance and forgiveness,
Under his wings,
He is my support,
His love will never run short.

WHEN EGYPT CALLS

I know you're saved,
I know you're filled,
I know you want to follow,
The Father's will;
But beware, Oh Precious child,
There's a war going on,
Know deep in your heart,
That you are a conqueror,
A Victor from the start.

But remember,
The enemy's tactics are ruthless—but subtle in scope;
He wants to deceive you,
Into thinking that you are strong on your own;
That in the time of temptation you don't need God,
That you are strong enough to cope.
Alone…without God.

So be careful my child when Egypt calls,
The sounds, the desires, the sights, the thoughts—
Not from God;
Satan remembers, as well as you do,
The things you once did,
With your old tired crew;
He knows just where to tempt, to poke, to coax,
Until you end up in despair, in sin, seemingly without hope.

So when Egypt calls,
Turn a deaf ear my child,
And call on my name—"Jesus"

I will always answer your cry;
I'll make a way of escape for you to walk therein;
And because I love you and you trust me,
I promise to deliver you from sin.

So when Egypt calls,

Don't answer.

NOT AGAIN

I never thought it could happen to me…
Not again.
I was running the course so well,
What happened?
Where did I go wrong?
Time the tale would tell;
I let this world beat me in;
I forgot that Jesus said,
He would help me win;
Instead I gave up and returned to sin.

It all seemed fine, harmless and fun;
Until one morning when I looked at the sun,
And my soul cried;
My heart could not hide,
The loneliness hurt and despair of sin,
With its consequences to be faced from without and within.

It happened to me,
I failed God again,
I lost the joy and peace within.

But at the point of almost being
Crushed by the weight of my sins,
I heard a quiet voice say,
"I love you, I died for you"
"Nothing can separate you from my love"
"I will forgive you again."
"If you only repent,"

So repent I did.
At the moment of honesty,
God's love came down and lifted me,
Above and beyond my sins;
God forgave me, loved me and reassured me,
That He is the Alpha, Omega
The beginning and the end;
And because He is the Author and Finisher of my
Faith,
He will go with me to the end.
So now there is no condemnation,
No matter how Satan may try to accuse and deceive;
Because I am in Christ Jesus and, He is in me.

GUILT

Guilt is a killer to all who are pure;
Guilt says:
"You'll never be good,"
"So live like you're dead,"
"You heard what I said!"
"Forget your dreams, your hopes will never come true,"
"Because you are forever a guilty, guilty, guilty you!"
"You are destined to live a life of self hatred, remorse and
shame;
"That fact nothing and no one can change."
So exhausted in despair from repeated "try's" and failures,
We choose to accept hopelessness as our fate
and believe—for us—it's too late…

BUT GUILT IS A LIAR!

An evil demon straight from hell;
Designed to destroy you,
Designed to rob you of your purpose,
Your peace,
Your belief,
That God loves you.

Guilt will try to make you believe that
You are no good,
Because of what you did;
That you deserve only junk;
Self loathing and hatred become your daily bread,
As the enemy whispers condemning lies into your head,
**Not the truth that you are *highly* favored by God
and eternally blessed.**

Your heart cries out,
"How can a holy God ever forgive me?"
But once you trust him and confess
Jesus Christ himself will give you the strength to repent

God's verdict is

NOT GUILTY!

"NOT GUILTY" is His decree;
You are not condemned in Christ Jesus—
in Christ you can be set free!

Sovereign, Holy, Compassionate God
Did this just
for
You,

Before the world was formed;
Before the world was formed.

So, for the disease of guilt and condemnation
The Great Physician prescribes:
"THERE IS THEREFORE NO CONDEMNATION FOR
THOSE WHO ARE IN CHRIST JESUS!"
"IT WAS FOR YOUR GUILT THAT I,
JESUS, WAS CRUCIFIED, BLED AND DIED!"

"I LOVE YOU!" says the LORD;
"TRUST my word;"
"FORGIVE YOURSELF!"

I will give you strength and love,
And take the gloom away,
You will see a brighter day!
I'll replace the gloom with peace, hope and confidence,
If in my presence you *choose* to stay;"

"So take my extended hand,
Just you and me,
Together we will walk into
Your
Special
Destiny…"

JUST A MINUTE…

Just for a minute.
I want to step out of my life. Take a
giant step to the

Left   or   Right.

Sometimes I just wanna take flight.

And soar far above my life;

Say goodbye to the strife.

Lord, give my spirit wings,

When life cuts like a knife.

GOODBYE...HELLO

the final curtain call has come,
life is ebbing away underneath the evening sun,
i lived a life,
life lived me,
<u>Sunrise Sunset</u>
i tried—i cried
on my tombstone
it will read.

goodbye...

I must be *insane!*
Only the enemy of my soul is to blame.
As long as there is life
There is HOPE!
As long as there is CHRIST
There is HOPE!

Forget death!
Forget goodbye!
Hope, New Day
I Love you life—4ever!

Hello Life!

HELLO!!!!!

I NEED A DRINK

Anger and Hostility Rage within
Triggered by a whim
Reminders of the burning inferno
Raging within
Explosions of emotion

I need a drink
I'm headed toward the brink
Emotions so high
Reason has left, can barely think

I need a drink
I'm at the brink
Emotions so high
I can't think

I need a drink
Crossed over the brink
Emotions run high
Pulsing in my head
Can't think

I need a drink—now
A drink from the living waters
My soul and spirit are parched
Panting for you Lord
I'm thirsty for your peace
I'M DYING FOR A DRINK!

Drown me in the living waters of Your Love
Jesus!!!
Immerse me in your presence
I'm passed the brink

I need a drink from the living waters
The waters from your well
To cool my parched, thirsty soul

Joy and peace return
As I drink and drink and drink and drink and drink
From the well that never runs dry...
From the well that *never runs dry*
Do you need a drink?

A PLACE FOR ME

When life at home becomes a losing battle—
You fall short;
When your Christian life is marked with failure and defeat—
Despite successes;
When life in the church becomes one exposure of
vulnerabilities after another—Judged;
You talk, you pray, you read, you fast, you determine;
But you still miss the mark, you don't measure up,
You fall short,
You begin to despair;
Tell me,

Where do you go?

The agony runs too deep—lasts too long;
Sometimes it hurts to be me;
Life can become a series of consequences, with little relief
Financial ruin, physical decay, spiritual bankruptcy, social
misfit, emotionally scarred, mental delay—
The list goes on…
Sometimes comparing myself to the homeless,
Or the world's population below the poverty line
Just to feel good, viable and alive;
Sometimes feeling below the bottom rung—
Not much to show for your life;
No place to be.

It hurts to be and not to be—
In the place I would/should/could be.
Why am I not there?
The gnawing echo of my heart, soul and mind.

The "process" has left my soul weary;
No energy left to pursue my dreams, my purpose—my
destiny;
Faith begins to shatter, confidence lost;
I've counted the cost (and come up short)
Now what do I do?
Where is there a place for me?
Where is there a place for me?
To rest my weary head?
Where is my space, my place?
My land promised?
Where do I fit? Where is my home?

Where do I fit?

My soul cries.

But amid the quandary of my heart, soul and mind,
Despite the unanswered questions of my soul,
I find one, solitary place.
I am safe in God's space.
I am welcomed into his outstretched, loving, eternal arms;

By Him, I am accepted—never rejected—despite
inadequacies.
I have one special place,
For me to be me;
Home
In God's Heart
Sometimes,
The only place
For me…

SHOOTING THE "J"

Conflict

I want to scream inside.
Pastor, What do you do?
When there's no male presence in your home,
To provide the male example and guidance that this sermon prescribes;
What happens to my children—do their hopes and dreams die?
Help, Help, Help I'm a single mother drowning!
Don't you see me?
I'm bleeding!
Don't you care?
I'm about to flat line…
But nobody knows, nobody sees
Because my bleeding is inside.
I'm lonely, abused, exhausted, depressed and at times confused;
I can't block out life,
The x-factor has caused so much strife;
The x-factor has killed and crushed my spirit,
Who will lift me up?

Who will lift up my children and me?
Jesus…I'm a woman infirmed
Like the woman in the parable;
I can't help myself, by myself;
I can't straighten up my back
I'm too bent over;
I can't even lift my head;
My faith is not enough to lift me up—it's so faint…

What do you do when the faith won't come?
When I'm too bent over,
Due to decades of infirmity,
Like the woman in the parable;
18 years of infirmity.
I can't look up;
I can't believe;

What do I do?
I'm crying on my bent, broken, knees…
Jesus, saints, church, please help me!
So I can look into the face of Jesus;
So I can believe too;
I have a speck of faith—but I still need your help,
Don't leave me alone;
I'm bleeding to death from the fiery darts;
I look like Jesus did in the Passion of the,
Christ…On the inside.

Church you are my last stop.

My last hope.
Don't leave it up to me to pull myself up by my own
"Bootstraps;"
I'm rejected, abandoned, forlorn, thrown away, and mixed up;
Strength to pull myself up is all gone…

Church, Pastors, Counselors, Saints and Family
When a person is bleeding,
First you have to stop the bleeding;
First you have to perform CPR,
Before healing and recovery can begin.

Church, Pastors, Jesus…someone!
Stop my bleeding!
Stop the crushing of my soul and
Then I can, I will believe, have faith and fight!

I'm screaming inside because of the pain,
Does anybody hear me? See me?
Pastor, Elder, Minister, Mother, Father, Friend

Do you hear my scream?

Can't Jesus show you my pain?
It's just me and Jesus,
Just the same.

He asked you,
Yes you, who are spiritual,
To loose me of my grave clothes,
And set me free!
Graves clothes of abuse self-hatred, self-destruction, slander,
    Dishonor…pain;
I need more than what you are giving,
I need your help, just the same,
Lift up your head,
Point me to Jesus,
Lift up my arms,
Help me lift them
So I can worship God too!

I need help!
I can't loose myself!
Do you hear me?
Look at the infirmed woman in the parable,
She couldn't loose herself.
Church, *please*, be moved with compassion
Not moved with blame…

RESOLUTION

Well if no one is around,
Will I and my children die?
My spirit deep inside faintly yells,
No, No, No!

I will get up off the ground;
I'm barely able to encourage myself,
But in pain, through pain I purpose to open my mouth,
I cry, "I worship you Lord!'
I finally say;
I will be renewed, restored and freed!
I say it, even if I don't feel it,
Through God's grace and strength,
The Blood of Jesus presides;
By His Love, His Word, His Command,
I will renew my walk,
I will get up and walk by faith,

Not by sight!
So get up—Myself,
Myself, get up and walk
Just walk by faith;

Jesus has the master plan;
Just keep holding his hand;
Your destiny is to be loosed not bound;
Your destiny is to get up;
Stop asking why,
Your destiny is to live...not die!

Infirmed Woman, mother, man or child Jesus says,
Thou Art Loosed!
In the Name of Jesus
Get Up!!!
Get Up!!
Get Up!

The Beginning.

This poem was inspired by a sermon of Bishop, Carlton T. Brown of Bethel Gospel Assembly called," Shoot the J"— which means shooting the jump shot of life. The crux of the message was that fathers and concerned men help their sons, boys and young men in their communities navigate life and "Shoot the J." As a woman and single parent I wondered who would help mentor my twin sons and help them "Shoot the J!"

MIDNIGHT LOVE

Thank you for your love
Thank you for caring and being there Lord;
When I thought it was the end,
When I could not find a friend,
You were there;
In the middle of the night,
When my soul was in the heat of the fight,
You caused my spirit to soar,
And take flight,
In the middle of the night.

Now it's morning...
I survived the turmoil of the night
And you Lord,
Made everything all right!

Eternal
Thank you...

Your Child _____

GREAT INSPIRATIONS: ORDINARY PEOPLE EXTRAORDINARY GOD

For I am persuaded, that neither death, nor life, nor angels, nor principalities, nor powers, nor things present, nor things to come, nor height, nor depth, nor any other creature, shall be able to separate us from the love of God, which is in Christ Jesus our LORD.

Romans 8:38, 39

...Hitherto hath the LORD helped us.

I Samuel 7:12

I am doing a great work, so that I cannot come down…

Nehemiah 6:3

FAITH

I can see her on the top floor,
of an old decaying brownstone,
in El Barrio, in poverty,
in the middle of hopelessness;
teaching as through she were in a great,
symposium or amphitheater;
giving her all,
while dodging drops from a leaking ceiling.

Teaching above the cries of a hungry baby,
or a battered wife,
teaching above the roar of drug traffic,
street gangs and crime just outside;
not allowing the noises of the ghetto,
to distract her or her audience—
but instead used them as examples of why
Christ had to die.

Her audience did not consist of great scholars with PhD's,
yet,
she treated each with pride, dignity and respect,
no matter what the intellect;
to Faith Brown all urban Christian youth
were royalty—the Kings kids,
with Christlike eyes, she saw potential,
worth and importance,
inside those who society despised.

Faith's message was simple;
her sermon John 3:16
because God so loved the world—that he gave
so that people could be free;
if we accept God's sacrifice—Christ
we can take our place in the kingdom
as God ordained it to be.

Now I see the students at the edge of their seats,
drinking in each drop as

Faith taught in her own easy, direct
yet humorous way,
about the Lordship of Jesus Christ;
that salvation is free but not cheap;
God sacrificed his only Son,
so expect suffering in this Christian race as we run.

Faith also taught self acceptance
not to deny our humanity,
she shared her feelings, her disappointments,
her anger, her pain,
                                    ...but eventually her calm,
while adjusting the scarf on her chemo
balding head;
she reminded us that we are God's creation of beauty,
not misery.

She reminded us to be alive
was not to be dead.

I also see Colorado born Faith
in the mountains of Camp Champion;
where she taught us teens of every color and nationality,
to appreciate the beauty of God's creativity;
as we hiked, (or rather stumbled)
soaking wet,
while she reminded us that Christ paid our debt,
through muddy insect filled swamps
on stony, treacherous trails in the rain,
as she continued to train us,
that salvation is free but not cheap,
we are gonna have to work our faith to stay free,
while we dodged the branches of maple, oak and
pine trees.

In all Faith did Christ was first and foremost to defend,
then other's lives came next,
her life she placed at the end;
she understood that God comforts us to comfort others,

she lived it, it was more than just words from her mouth;
she realized that God was no respecter of persons,
so that the church had no right to be.
Faith continually interceded for the world's holistic freedom
both actually and spiritually on bended knee.

Faith may no longer be here;
sadly, a purple satin sash of remembrance draped
her pulpit chair;
But be assured,
Faith will be surprised at all the stars in her crown,
for lives she touched, like mine...
awarded because of the time she took to care,
and let men know that God's love is near.

We salute you Faith Brown!
for you joined that great cloud of witnesses,
as you see the Savior's blessed face,
cheering us on as we run the this Christian race...

Author's Note:

This poem was dedicated to the memory of Dr. Rev. Faith Brown, one of my Christian mentors/educators who has inspired my life as a teenager and young adult. Faith Brown was an intergral part of Teen Challenge, was the founder of "Urban Youth Alliance" youth ministries located in New York City originally housed in Bethel Gospel Assembly in Harlem, New York. Rev. Brown originally from Colorado, followed the Lord to Fox Street in the South Bronx, where she ministered to drug dealers, gang leaders and their families throughout the 70's and later in" El Barrio" until she died of cancer in the late 80's. As founder of Urban Youth Alliance she enabled urban Christian young people in college and high school to establish Christian Clubs, fondly known as "Seekers", to share Christ with their friends throughout the city and to care for others throughout the world for Christ. She supported organizations such as Bread for the World and fought against injustice, discrimination, illiteracy and poverty. The legacy of Faith Brown continues in Urban Youth Alliance today.

THE MAN

Ezra Nehemiah is his name,
Rebuilding the walls of ruined lives is his
game,
His message is straight,
Jesus Christ is the only gate,
For mankind the penalty of death to escape;
As Bethel's Emeritus scribe and priest
He teaches that salvation is free but not cheap.

But away from the pulpit,
When Sundays are gone;
On Mondays, Tuesdays, morning or night,
During everyday life;
He practices what he preaches,
With his life he reaches,
And touches everyone with his God given love.

Admiration, greatness and respect
Are not strong enough
To express what I feel;
For this great man of God;
Great man of men;
Who is man enough to cry,
For his people—his flock—entrusted to him
by God...
He's strong enough to be gentle,
Great enough to identify with the tiniest child.
(Who knows he keeps a candy jar just for them.)

He knows how and when to laugh,
(Just watch him preach)
When to frown,
When to smile,
When to sympathize,
When to act,
When to pray,
When to discipline,
When to restore,
While creating an atmosphere in Bethel.
Where all can enjoy Jesus more.

Giving yourself unselfishly to others is his creed;
Humility he wears as a comfortable, familiar cloak.

"Hitherto hath the Lord helped us"
Is his motto;
Demonstrating love is his creed;
Touched, he cries at communion, each time;
When reminded of how Christ was betrayed,
And how brutally Christ died—for us,
How Christ's demonstration of love
Paved the way,
For our freedom,
Christ shed His blood,
For all men to be free.

So with the love of Christ,
Bishop past three score and ten
Preservers through every "Perfect Storm" of life,
With laughter, wisdom and God's grace,
He remains in the race,
Until the day God usheres him into the eternal
sunshine,
To dwell with Him in spectacular splendor
Forevermore.

He smiles to himself,
Fulfillment sublime,
Both states the same,
"To live is Christ"
but
"To die is gain!"

Author's Note:

The previous poem was dedicated to the memory of Dr. Bishop Emeritus Ezra Nehemiah Williams, former Senior Pastor of Bethel Gospel Assembly for over three decades, located in Harlem, New York. Bishop Ezra was my pastor during the major seasons of my life as a child, teenage, young adult, single mother and mature adult. He inspired me to greatness with his humble determination to serve God and help humanity at all costs. It was this inspiration and encouragement that caused me to write this poetry book. For almost three decades, my poems were featured in our church's newsletter, "The Bethel's Voice", Bishop Williams saved my poetry because I would always give him a personal copy. One day, after sharing a poem with him he said, "Ellie, you ought to put your poetry together in a collection.", I responded, "Yeah Pastor, and I'll call the book "From the Heart." That was almost 30 years ago. Unfortunately, he passed away to be with our Lord in August 2009 before this book was published. But I had the privilege of reading this poem to him personally and sharing my dedication to him before he died.

Bishop Ezra was also one of my spiritual mentors and educators who showed me the love of God not only in word but action. Bishop Williams was the Senior Pastor of Bethel Gospel Assembly, the "Loving, Learning and Launching Church" located in the heart of Harlem for over four decades. Under his leadership this church has established and maintained its position in the community as a "Hospital in Harlem" rebuilding the walls and lives of broken men, women and children through the vehicle of love. Bethel's global as well as domestic vision of love, hope and restoration for all people God was birthed inside the heart of Bishop Ezra N. Williams. This vision and legacy has been transplanted and continues to thrive in Bethel under the current leadership of Bishop Carlton T. Brown, who also was inspired by this great man's life.

A PRESIDENCY—AGAINST ALL ODDS!

The revolution was televised in techno color today;
Downloaded from CNN and the hearts and minds of
All Americans,
We were one today.

As we witnessed hope, promise, and ideological
Transition,
That affected every rural" hamlet" to urban "street corner"
From welfare to Wall Street,
As students watched history in the making
Sons and Daughters watched,
America in her glory;
Our greatness has come…

From the rubble of economic, social, moral and geological
despair we arise
Tears of pride in each American eye
As we witnessed the inauguration of

Barack Hussein Obama,
Our Nations' 43rd and 44th President.

I too can tell my child, "One day you can become President!"

America, we did it!
With faith and hope in God,
We met the challenges and did not succumb to fear,

We've elected and inaugurated our first African American
President
We accomplished it—
Against All Odds!

America let us strive to stand together,
For generations to come,
Hand in Hand,
Heart to Heart,

Let Freedom Ring!

REFLECTIONS

And God said, Let us make man in our image...
And God saw everything that he had made...
and behold it was good.

Genesis 2:26, 31

WHO AM I?

I look in the mirror,
What do I see?
Is the reflection in that glass somebody else?
While I look I feel outside myself,
As I wonder who is this reflection?
Is this me?
Am I really alive?
Or is this a dream that will soon die?

My life is superimposed within my body,
And my lifestyle is superimposed with that,
But I wonder if the totality of my being
Is found in the exterior of my interior;

Am I only an aimless body fulfilling a lifestyle?
Just a liaison with the maze and race called life?

Well if I am
Then—I have no reason to reason,
No thoughts to think,
No feelings to feel,
No dreams to dream
No hope to hope.

Then—I would be sentenced to a life of
Interior
Emptiness,
Condemned to a hollow shell,
Just moving around as the wave of life moves me…

But I must be more than this!

Within me I find the ability,
To reason,
To think,
To feel,
To dream and
To hope…

I am more than a series of movements,
Caused by the physiological metabolic and
Equilibrium systems of my body.

I have a mind that thinks fantastic thoughts,
Contained within me is a heart with the capacity
To feel, cry and love;
I even catch my spirit hoping and striving
To reach high above;
All of these actions and reactions to the
Stimuli of Life,

This is me.

I am a conglomerate of mixed emotions balanced amid
Creative ideas and ardent beliefs;
I'm more than a lifeless fleshly sepulcher;
My life is a special, unique and separate entity,
In the sea of life;
I'm a beautiful fish in that sea,
Not debris that moves along with the whims of the Tide;
As I look in the mirror with myself I confide.

This is the me that I've longed to find,
And who I finally found;
I love "me", the real "me."
Even if the world never sees "me."

Because "me" is the best thing
That I Could Ever Be.

TEACH ME LORD

Teach me to love
As I live everyday
Teach me to see
Yield and forgive
Father I need you that's why I pray.

Teach me to know your voice and your will
Help me to climb my own special hill
You have the plan
So help me to see
The plan
You have for me.

Teach me Oh Lord
How I pray
Lord today
Teach me Lord.

SPECIAL AND BLESSED

I'm glad I'm me!
I would not want to be anyone else
But me.
My life is full of valleys and peaks,
And seemingly uncrossable seas;
Insurmountable odds surround me,
But with God's constant care, involvement and love
Which only comes from above
I stay on course.

Despite loss, disappointment or mistakes,
God's loving hand guides me and leads me
From level to level,
Peak to peak,
Until I reach the top of each mountain;
The summit of my dreams;
The peak of purpose and destiny,
God makes reality of my dreams.

I'm your trophy
For all the world and heaven to see;
I owe it all to you Lord,

Thank you for my destiny!

Again, thank you Lord for making me—me,
There's no other person that I'd rather be;

Eternal Thank You.

THE GOD OF "AFTER"

I serve a god of "After"
Not just "Before"
He encourages my heart
Through His timely Word—
God makes my heart soar.

He encourages me to believe
That his promises are true;
That my "After" day is coming
Even if today—trials and suffering
Make me blue.

Life in Christ brings light
And dispels darkness and gloom
Jesus is my light,
At the end of my tunnel,
My destiny is secure,
Because the God I serve
Is the God of "After"
Not just "Before."

****

Look at my makeover;
Surprise!
I'm starting to resemble Jesus.
Thank you God for my "After."
For a while it seemed like it would never come;
But come it did!
God promised and He delivered.
It was worth the suffering, pain, struggle and fight!
I had to walk by faith not by sight…

So don't get caught up in "Before"
My dear Christian friend,
Your "After" is around the corner, too;
The suffering and dark days of your "Before"
Are destined to End.

Welcome to "After"
We've been waiting for You!

GLISTENING IN THE BRONX

I saw the sun glisten on the waves today;
As the waves giggled and danced
across the sea,
I saw the sun glisten on the waves today;
Shinning brightly—gloriously blinding me,
Yet I continued to stare,
At the sun glistening on the waves,
That warmed my heart,
And illumined my soul.

The sweet sea breeze,
Blew through my hair,
Blew through the gloom,
Blew the clouds away.

I saw the sun glisten on the waves today;
Against the fray I fought to stay,
I fought the traffic of tragedy, violence, urban concrete
jungle…death.

I pushed through barriers of turmoil and pain,
And was rewarded with the scenery of serenity,
Pastel colored boats,
Gently rocking to the rhythm of the sea,
Dancing on top the sun soaked blue waves,
Tranquility arrested my soul;
As I watched,
I smiled…

I saw the sun glisten on the waves today…

Did you?

AFFAIRS OF THE HEART...

You have kept count of my tossings and put my tears in a bottle...

Proverbs 15:13

*He hath send me to bind up the brokenhearted
...to give unto them beauty for ashes,
the oil of joy for mourning,
the garment of praise for the spirit of heaviness*

Isaiah 61:1,3

YOU MADE ME LAUGH…AND CRY

You made me laugh,
You made me cry,
Now all that's left
Is the reason why;
The truth is known,
The future's now,
Our love is lost
And can never be found;
What took it's place
Is pain and despair
Can peace be found anywhere?

Thoughts run over and over in my mind
How, When, Why did
I get replaced?
How did I get left behind?

Now I know the truth
To me you lied.
The
well is dry
The
day is old
our relationship has become
tarnished, fake gold.

I showed you love,
You showed you didn't care.

I spoke to you in sweetness,
You spoke to me with indifference and lies.

I proved to you that I was a woman
in your corner—by your side,
You proved to me that you were not
worthy of my love.

I touched you with devotion,
You touched me with deception;

It hurt.

You shot deadly arrows of rejection
and abandonment,
That pierced my exposed soul
And penetrated
My heart until it bled.
You threw me out and left me for dead.

The pain went so deep,
Better company with you never to keep,
Than to feel my heart weep;
Too hurt to count sheep
Cried to God to ease my pain—to sleep.

Only God's presence
each night;
Relieved my splintered,
Like broken glass,
ripped through my raw
heart soul.

God came in Holy Spirit doses,
Each night at 1 0'clock,
Each night at 2 0'clock,
Each night at 3 o'clock,
Until sunrise,
Until sleep would come.

Sometimes wondered if death would relieve the pain?
Grief too familiar,
Too many broken
/severed/
Relationships,

layers of brokenness
a nightmare that never ends...
How much pain can one heart stand?
and beat?
and live?

I hurt.

But...
Through my tears.
Through my fears.
I prayed that one day soon,
Like a butterfly I would be free,
No longer in a dark cocoon,
Filled with heartache and gloom;
But free to fly gracefully,
Gently, through the flowered countryside
And land on a beautiful, endearing,
Benevolent fragranced flower,
Where I will find my place
In a wholesome space,
Free to laugh and love again...

Thank God

Without

You.

THE DAY I SAID NO!

The day I told you NO

Was a liberating day

NO to ill treatment and disrespect

NO to always *your* way

NO consideration of mine

NO to you treating me unkind

NO to the waiting, disappointment and

tears

NO to your unconcern and lack of care

NO to you not seeing me for who I am

NO to you making my heart sad

NO to this time and that time and the other time

When you made me feel like less

Respect is my only quest

NO

I'm not taking it anymore

Learn how to love and respect me

Or walk out the door.

NEVER AGAIN

It's been a long time coming,
I thought we would never end;
But I was deceived
To think we would wed
You pretended to the end!

For so many years
Repeating the same tragic mistake
An unending cycle of false hope and misery
I realized I had believed lies
So I sat myself down
And I asked myself why
Why? Do I believe lies?

Loneliness and fear are a deadly combination;
Emotions can influence you
To make detrimental decisions,
To make costly choices that destroy you,
God's precious creation.

Now, I understand the pain and price of disobedience,
When you become unequally yoked with an unbeliever
A covenant with disaster;
Sooner or later
Your life, spirit and purpose become choked.
You end up empty, alone—yearning
For God's peace in mercy to send
As you slowly, painfully wait for your severed heart to mend.
"It's just not worth it!"
As I lift my voice to heaven with bitter,
sorrowful tears in my eyes,

Only viable solution is to yield and trust God;
Then finally resolve;
It's over. All over.
Lord, my Redeemer
Never again.
By your grace and my choice,
I will obey your voice;
I will let your love fill every void.
Fill *every* void.

So, pain and heartache, *don't* get it twisted—**I'M DONE!**

JESUS WHAT YOU MEAN TO ME

Jesus you have been there
Every step of the way;
To tell and show that you love me,
"My precious child, trust and obey,"
At times I behaved like your love didn't matter;
I took your love for granted;
I let your love wait;
But I was wrong.
To ever think I could find love in
Any other place or face
But in your eyes Lord,
In your loving, endearing, truthful face;
I'm wrapped up in your outstretched arms;
You mean everything to me;
I can't help but worship you,
From deep inside my healing heart,
Mended by your unending, unconditional,
undying Love;
Thank you Jesus for your staunch faithfulness,
Loving kindness and tender mercy;
You Jesus, You alone are real.
You have proven you are the Truth and the Light;
You bring me joy and hope,
You demolish inner strife;
Thank you for not giving up on me
Nor giving me more than I can bear—
Despite my tears;
But with each and every burden you did share;
I love you Lord—You are beautiful,
Your love is perfect;
Your depth of care,
No man can compare!

A PRAYER FOR INTIMACY

O' Lord, I want to be in your presence
In the secret place of your heart
Where the world is shut outside the door
Of my prayer closet
The center of your love.

O' Lord, I'm standing, naked
in the threshold;
Lord let me in,
To the secret place of the most high
Where you precious spirit dwells within
Lord, the cares, the fears, the affairs
Of this world
The conflicting internal desires
Threaten to keep me from entering in
Remove them Lord
I shut the world out
I quiet my soul
I close my complaining mouth…

To commune with the one who lovingly bids me come
To commune with you Lord
In the secret prayer closet within my heart
A place prepared for us.

A place prepared for you
As I allow you to reign and occupy the throne of my heart
As I humbly bow and enter in
To eternal communion, eternal love

Whisk me away, Father
Into the celestial heaven above
Each time I enter into the secret prayer
Closet of you love
Each time I enter into the secret place
For me and you to share
The intimacy of Divine Love
Lord I desire to forever meet you there…

FALLING OUT OF THE ABYSS

i'm falling in the Abyss,
i clutch the sides to stop my fall,
but alas, to no avail,
my hands slide down the grimy walls,
help me!—i cry;
i tripped over the edge
and i'm helplessly
falling,
falling,
falling…

Then Love appears—
Out of nowhere
Love reaches out and Rescues Me!
Love holds me tight,
Doesn't let go,
As Love flies me out—against the desires of the
dark abyss;
We fly upward through gravity—through
the clutches of darkness;
Love pulls me through the quicksand
of pain and wickedness—as we fly…

I watch sin by the wayside,
as Love lifts me all the way out
of the dark, destructive, doomed pit;
Through the quicksand of deception and
wickedness
covering the mouth of the hole;
Then Jesus set my feet on a Rock Foundation,

Christ the Solid Rock;
Love's plateau of Hope, Power, Faith and Trust
God's love in Christ's hand
that rescued Me!
That *Never* lets go!
Love that holds on tight!
Love that declares to my soul
I GOT YOU!
I got you!
Never give up!
Hold tight!
Stay in the fight!
You will see the Light!

VICTIM TO VICTOR

And we know that <u>all</u> things work together for good to them that love God, to them who are the called according to his purpose.

Romans 8:28

No weapon formed against you shall prosper.

And I will give her her vineyards from thence, and the valley of Achor for a Door of Hope: And she shall sing there…

Hosea 2:15

INCEST

"SHHHHHHHH!"
"You better not tell *anyone*—OR ELSE!"
the 6ft giant man said.

i'm a helpless child
orphaned then adopted

"Come here sweet child"

Uncle, why are you touching me…
there?

Does anyone see?

Does anyone hear?

Does anyone care?

You're crushing my innocence
i can't stop you.
i'm frozen, paralyzed and scared with fear
When,
"You better not tell anyone"
echoes in my 8 year old tiny ears.

My screams are choked by your nasty tongue
and fear;
What are these sensations?
I feel guilty, dirty—like *I* did something wrong.
My screams are swallowed

No one hears,
Inside this dark, forbidden basement
No one knows.
so *it* continues…
i'm filled with fright
when i visit during the day or night.

~~~~~~~~~~

The child of incest suffers…alone.

I'll bury my cry deep inside;
So deep that I'll never
remember,
I'll force myself to forget.
I'll bury the violation, victimization and my helpless
unheard cries,
Deep, so deep inside…
Until one day…decades away…
When violation matures into
volcanic, internal rage
that later destroys self,
the self that let itself
be violated.

Self destruction comes in many forms:
drug abuse to ease the pain,
chosing the abuser in each relationship the same,
domestic violence, mental and
emotional abuse become the order of the
day;

Anger and rage reversed on self—by self
Because someone has to pay
Someone is to blame;
sadistic behavior is the remedy
self mutilation hoping to relieve the pain
alcohol—to remove the shame, guilt stain—
overeating to feel good again,
lover after lover—never-learned-how to say "no"
paralyzed again and again,
learned about sex from childhood incest;
The cruel world says,
"The victim is to blame!"
the adult child believes the same.
"So keep hurting yourself"
"You're worthless"
Yells the voice inside your head.

but

One day **Jesus** reached down
and picked up the damaged child
inside;
Held her,
Loved her,
Wiped the tears from her eyes,
and her heart...
Christ love expressed by the shedding of his blood
for all sexual abuse,
for *your*s too,
Jesus heard my screams, took the sting and shame of incest away...

Only Christ can take the violation of incest and rape
away,
And replace it with
"I love you!"
"You are the apple of my eye!"
"You are valuable, full of worth
that's why I died;"
"You are fearfully and wonderfully made!"
"Now share my love with others!"
"You are set free from abuse today!"

"You *are* set free from *all* abuse today!"

DOMESTIC VIOLENCE—THE CYCLE CONTINUES…

"I'm sorry, it will never happen again."
"I love you."

That's what my baby's daddy said.

While in the ambulance, those words swirled around my head.
Eight months pregnant beaten up from sunrise to night,
kicked me where his baby lied inside,
All because of jealous rage
When will my life turn the page?

I love him.
He said he loved me.
But why should love hurt?

Who can I talk to?
I'm so ashamed,
Afraid to press charges,
Scared he'll come back and beat me again.

I later took him back—
to my shame.
I didn't want to raise my baby alone.
Anyway, he'll change it won't take long…

The cycle of domestic violence
sometimes never ends
until at her funeral
we say our last
Amen.

FORGIVENESS

"Hurt people, Hurt people"
I heard someone say;
So, I forgive you for what you've done.
I release you from my prison
I release you from the bars of murder, payback, revenge,
bitterness, explanation and apology;
Because Jesus forgave and forgives me,
Over and over and over again.
How can I not forgive you?

Self I forgive you too!
I let you off the hook,
No more dept to be paid;
If Jesus could forgive me,
Then I can, will and do
Forgive me too;
I forgive myself,
Yes, you in the mirror,
I now awaken to a bright day anew…

Thank you for giving me the power and strength,
to do
what I tried so hard to do,
with all my might—still could not do—
Forgive…

I forgave only through Divine impartation.
Impartation of the heart and spirit of God.
Your forgiveness was imparted,
Deep inside my heart;

Dissolved the hurt and pain inside,
I let you God abide,
Hurt, from you I did not hide.
Now I can say—I forgive you.
All of you.

Surprise!

I'm free!

FREE AT LAST—TO BE…

Yes, I'm Free at last!
No more chains holding me!
Jesus completely freed me,
From the pain and nightmares of my past!
I'm Free at last!

Soaring high above,
My spirit soars on God's love…
I'm Free at last!
Jesus has forgiven and completely forgotten my past!
I'm Free at last!

You too can be Free at last;
Let Jesus in
He will forgive and forget your past
Then you will fly on His wings of love…

You too can be Freed from your past
Then you too can sing,
"I'm Free At Last!"
Jesus can help you move on,
Conquer and forget your past.

We are Free at Last!
Jesus took away our past!
Replaced our chains with wings!
Now our souls can sing!
Free at last!

Wait…

Listen carefully and you will hear
The Savior softly whisper in your ear,
I set you Free
So you can Be
All I created you To Be.

Remember, I was pierced on my side,
Wounded and Bruised
Bleeding for your Freedom.
For You I Died!

It is finished!

IT IS FINISHED!

My *precious* child
STAY FREE!

FREE AT LAST—*REPRISE*

Free at last!
Free at last!
Jesus freed me from my past!
Now My soul can sing—I'm Free at last!

Watch me soar like a dove!
Freed by the power of His love,
My heart soars far above,
On His wings of love.

Jesus forgave my sin,
Gave me peace within,
And Freed me from the pain of my past!
Now I'm Free at last.

If you let Jesus in,
He'll forgive your sin,
And Free you from the pain of your past!
Today your soul can sing—I'm Free at last!

Free at last!
Free at last!
Jesus Freed you from your past!
Now Your soul can sing—I'm Free at last!
You too can soar like a dove!
Freed by the power of His love,
Your heart can soar far above,
on His wings of love.
Free at last!
Free at last!

No more chains holding me!
Jesus Freed me from my past!
Free at last!
Free at last!
Jesus freed me from my past!
Now *My* soul can sing,
I'm Free at last!

LOVE IS…FOREVER!

i may be able to speak any language from here or above
the Bible says,
but it all means nothing if i don't have Love;
even if i can understand all secrets and hidden mysteries of
mankind,
i'm lost,
if the hidden mystery of Love i can't find;
my faith may be able to move gigantic mountains,
high into the sky,
but without Love
my faith would surely die;
without love my "sacrifice"
would be a lie.

Love never gives up;
it is true—not corrupt;
Love is *always* kind,
Love doesn't find itself important—but others—in its own
mind.

Love doesn't remember the suffering or pain,
that comes from being hurt by someone,
because with God and understanding the victory
is won;
Love forgives;
Love let's others live.

Love is not happy with evil and sin,
but rejoices in truth from within;
Love isn't jealous or full of pride,

Love was displayed when Jesus Christ died;
Love looks for the best in a person to see;
Love is understanding, so it doesn't stay angry;
Love never thinks of itself,
Or constantly for its personal gain or wealth.

Love believes in all things;
Love hopes for all things;
Love keeps on loving in all things;
Love *keeps* on loving in all things;

Love will never come to an end...

I'M HEALED!

I stood at the altar,
With my hands lifted up,
With my heart lifted up,
With my voice lifted up.

I stood at the altar,
With fear dissolved,
As Jesus energized me with His power,
touched me with His love,
and engulfed me with His Presence,
Submerged me within His love.

I trembled as if an earthquake erupted inside,
Its depth reached those private, hidden,
Pain filled chambers of my heart and soul.

As God reached down—

I reached up—

We met in the atmosphere of Adoration, Praise and Worship,
In the dimension of released Divine healing,
Triggered by Your Divine love.
You healed me Lord.

You healed me in all the places where I hurt,
You healed me of my emotional and physical infirmity,
No longer bent down and crippled in pain,
You cause me to stand and stomp on Satan's head,

As I rejoiced in our Divine synthesis as you revealed yourself
to me,
Divine Purpose, Divine Love, Divine Ecstasy,
Beyond intoxication, good feeling or excitement—You
Healed Me!

I'm not afraid of the future or the past—I'm lost in you Jesus;
I'm living inside your Presence—You live inside of me;
I stand behind the Lion of Judah—I am not alone, Never alone!
No matter how cold the winter may seem,
Made frigid by the brutal winds of adversity.

You healed me at the altar with the melting warmth of Divine
Love,
I walked away a new creature, with new legs, new hope,
New strength, new resolve—more than just a zapping—
Divine Love…
Will you be healed today?

VICTORY...IS ON THE HORIZON!

Look beyond your troubles
Look beyond your fears
You don't have to be discouraged
Let Jesus wipe away your tears
For just on the horizon
Victory's about to dawn
So get up and praise Him
Why be gloomy and forlorn?

For Jesus is the God of the brokenhearted
For crushed and broken spirits He came
So let Jesus into your heart and
Where you hurt
Let Him share and bear your pain
Jesus is touched with the feelings of our infirmities
His love and power will keep you sane.

Remember, victory is on the horizon
It's just beyond the dawn
Whatever the situation is
Trust Christ to pull you up over the top
Of the hill you're destined to climb
You can see clearly
You can see the SONshine!

H.O.P.E.

I hope that these words bring you
healing
from the wounds of life;
I hope that you will not give up
But take hope for a brand new start;
But most of all,
I hope that you let Christ's love
completely heal your heart.

H.O.P.E.

is what I pray for you
today

**Christ's
Healing
Of
People Everywhere!**

Is what my book
"From the Heart"
endeavors to say.

GOD BLESS YOU!

FROM HIS HEART ♥

Dear Beloved,

For God So Loved The World
That He Gave His Only
Begotten Son
That Whosoever Believeth
In Him
Shall Not Perish
But Have Everlasting
Life…
(John 3:16)

From My Heart♥

With Love,

Jesus…
the one who died.
For You!

♥ *(If you believed and accepted the Lord into you heart*
e-mail me at egheart2@gmail.com so I can pray and rejoice
with you!) ♥

THE

BEGINNING...

ACKNOWLEDGEMENTS

This book could never have been completed without the love and support of the God placed people in my life. I express to each of you my deepest gratitude for your love, encouragement and the confidence you have in me. Thank you for your continuous acknowledgment and validation of the expressive, creative light "bright as the sun" (the meaning of Eleanor) that God has created inside me...

First, to my Lord, Savior and soon coming King, Jesus Christ *who relentlessly pursued me with his undying, unconditional love and has not allowed His purposes for my existence to be thwarted by anything or anyone in this life...*

To my parents, Anna and the late Alphonso George your steadfast, tough love, faithfulness and laughter has kept me sailing...

To my daughter Dejshona, you are my eternal breath of fresh air, My wonderful, remarkable, beautiful reflection... You inspire me to greatness...

To my son Michael, you are the strongest, truest and bravest man that I know, you unyielding confidence in your Creator challenges me to holiness and excellence...
You are forever beloved...

To my son Matthew, you seemingly infinite intellect, giftedness and brilliance beckons me to unfathomable depths with tears of joy. Your humor and love brings a laugh to my soul...
You are my gift...

To the late Dr. Bishop Emeritus Ezra N. Williams, who planted the seed of this book inside my heart over two decades ago and encouraged me to greatness...

To my Senior Pastor Bishop Carlton T. Brown, whose patient love and deep understanding continuously believed in me—when I could not believe in myself...

To Reverend Lorna Brown, who tenaciously would not let God's promise of authorship die inside of me, despite numerous obstacles,
You encouraged me to believe in a God greater than my circumstances...(or excuses...)

To Dr. Doreen Stewart, who guided this project to the doorsteps of destiny and has demonstrated the depths of agape friendship, sisterhood and profound sacrifical love...
I'm the product of your faithfulness, prayers and tears...
You share in my success girlfriend!

To Reverend Joyce Eady, who viewed me through God's eyes and beckoned me to view myself through Christ's lens and rejoice in God's creation of me...

To Reverend Wendie Trott, who encouraged me beyond myself into God's glory to help me breathe heaven's air...

To Reverend Ruth Ann Wynter, who spoke a word into my soul to never again apologize for the gifts, talents and abilities God created inside of me...but function in my purpose to the glory of God...

To my cousin Laura Ann Young, God used you to be my safe haven in the middle of the chaos, for my wounded heart and soul, you treated me like royalty...

To Rhonda Fleming, who jumped started this project over fi ve years ago with your personal time, love and professionalism...

To Ben Walker, whose artistic expertise created visual life for my words.

To the numerous editors and proofreaders who took the time to read each word Iona Allen, Zuri Mckeever, Rev. Avril Deuwson, Reverend Wendy Trott and Deacon Duane Gallop.